An animal community

Bobbie Kalman

 Crabtree Publishing Company

www.crabtreebooks.com

Created by Bobbie Kalman

Author and Editor-in-Chief
Bobbie Kalman

Educational consultants
Elaine Hurst
Reagan Miller
Joan King

Editors
Joan King
Reagan Miller
Kathy Middleton

Proofreader
Crystal Sikkens

Design
Bobbie Kalman
Katherine Berti

Photo research
Bobbie Kalman

Production coordinator
Katherine Berti

Prepress technician
Katherine Berti

Photographs
Dreamstime: p. 18
iStockphoto: p. 15
All other photographs by Shutterstock

Library and Archives Canada Cataloguing in Publication

Kalman, Bobbie, 1947-
    An animal community / Bobbie Kalman.

(My world)
Includes index.
ISBN 978-0-7787-9446-2 (bound).--ISBN 978-0-7787-9490-5 (pbk.)

    1. Prairie dogs--Habitations--Juvenile literature.
I. Title. II. Series: My world (St. Catharines, Ont.).

QL737.R68K34 2010   j599.36'7   C2009-906105-8

Library of Congress Cataloging-in-Publication Data

Kalman, Bobbie.
  An animal community / Bobbie Kalman.
    p. cm. -- (My world)
  Includes index.
  ISBN 978-0-7787-9490-5 (pbk. : alk. paper) -- ISBN 978-0-7787-9446-2
(reinforced library binding : alk. paper)
  1. Prairie dogs--Juvenile literature. 2. Animal societies--Juvenile
literature. I. Title. II. Series.

  QL737.R68K35 2010
  599.36'71782--dc22
                                                        2009041224

Crabtree Publishing Company

www.crabtreebooks.com   1-800-387-7650

Printed in China/122009/CT20091009

Published in Canada
Crabtree Publishing
616 Welland Ave.
St. Catharines, Ontario
L2M 5V6

Published in the United States
Crabtree Publishing
PMB 59051
350 Fifth Avenue, 59th Floor
New York, New York 10118

Published in the United Kingdom
Crabtree Publishing
Maritime House
Basin Road North, Hove
BN41 1WR

Published in Australia
Crabtree Publishing
386 Mt. Alexander Rd.
Ascot Vale (Melbourne)
VIC 3032

What is in this book?

What is a community?   4

A prairie dog town   6

Sharing food   8

Prairie dog families   10

Community day care   12

Working together   14

Town guards   16

Prairie dog teachers   18

Communication   20

The rodent family   22

Words to know and Index   24

What is a community?

A **community** is a place.
It is also the group of **living things**
that shares that place.
Living things are plants,
animals, and people.
Prairie dogs are animals
that live in communities.
They live in communities
to stay alive.

prairie dogs

squirrel

Prairie dogs are not dogs.
They are a kind of squirrel.
(See pages 22–23.)

A prairie dog town

Prairie dogs live in big communities.
Their communities are called **towns**.

tunnel

Some towns are huge!
They are deep in the ground.
Towns have rooms and **tunnels**.

room

Sharing food

Communities share food.
Prairie dog communities
share food, too.

Prairie dog towns are on **prairies**.
Prairies are flat areas with
grasses, flowers, and other
plants growing on them.
Prairie dogs eat
these plants.

8

Prairie dogs eat the flowers and
other plants that grow on prairies.

Prairie dog families

Communities have families.
Prairie dog communities
also have families.
Prairie dog **pups**, or babies,
are born in the spring.
Prairie dog mothers feed their pups
milk from their bodies.

The pups stay
in their town
in a room
called a **nursery**.

When the pups are five weeks old,
they come above ground to look for food.

Community day care

Do you go to day care?

Prairie dog towns also have day care.

The mothers take turns looking after all the pups in one family.

They watch over the pups and make sure they are safe.

They also teach the pups which plants are good to eat.

Working together

The prairie dog community **cooperates**, or works together, to dig their towns. Digging a town is a big job!
Each prairie dog helps with the digging.

These prairie dogs are talking while they work.

Is this prairie dog stuck? Will he get out?

Town guards

Communities have police officers to protect people. Prairie dogs also protect their towns from **predators**. Predators are animals that hunt and eat other animals. Foxes, coyotes, and hawks eat prairie dogs.

coyote

fox

Prairie dog guards watch for predators, such as this hawk. They work together to keep their town safe.

hawk

Prairie dog teachers

Communities have schools where children learn from teachers. Prairie dog towns also have teachers. Adult prairie dogs teach the pups how to stay alive. They teach them how to find food, how to dig tunnels, and how to guard the town from predators.

This adult is teaching a pup how to stand guard.

Communication

Communities share information.
Sharing information is called **communication**.
Prairie dogs communicate in different ways.
They make loud calls to warn other prairie dogs of danger.
They use different sounds to warn about different predators.

People communicate love with hugs and kisses. Prairie dogs huddle and touch their front teeth together to greet one another.

The rodent family

People called prairie dogs "dogs" because they make barking sounds, but prairie dogs are not dogs. They belong to the **rodent** family. Rodents have four front teeth that never stop growing. The animals shown here are rodents that are like prairie dogs.

rodent teeth

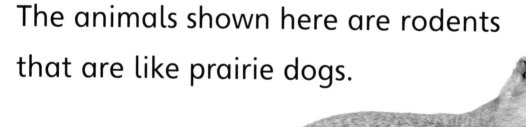

ground squirrel

marmot

tree squirrel

chipmunk

Words to know and Index

communication
pages 20–21

cooperation
pages 14–15

families
pages 10–11, 12

food pages
8–9, 11, 18

guards pages
16–17, 18, 19

predators pages
16, 17, 18, 20

pups pages
10, 11, 12, 18, 19

rodents
pages 22–23

towns pages
6–7, 8, 10, 12,
14, 16, 17, 18